A Song On the Road Home

A Collection of Spirtual Poems

H.N. Lawrence

M&B Global Solutions Inc.
Green Bay, Wisconsin (USA)

A Song on the Road Home
A Collection of Spirtual Poems

© 2022 H. Nicole Lawrence

First Edition
All Rights Reserved. The author grants no assignable permission to reproduce for resale or redistribution. This license is limited to the individual purchaser and does not extend to others. Permission to reproduce these materials for any other purpose must be obtained in writing from the publisher except for the use of brief quotations.

Cover photo © 2015 H.N. Lawrence

ISBN: 978-1-942731-41-2

Published by M&B Global Solutions Inc.
Green Bay, Wisconsin (USA)

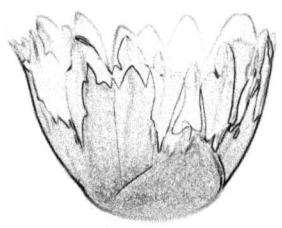

Dedication

*To my spiritual teachers, both western and from the East.
At times, they had a rough piece of clay to work with,
but they managed to shape me and help me grow.*

Contents

Introduction 1

Section 1 .... **3**
Life Changing Hands 5
Your Light 6
Moving Unseen 7
Expansion 8
Gaze 9
Heart Blossom 10
Unraveling 11
Cannot Go Back 12
Hour 13
Loved One 14
Tender Touch 15
Wind of Unknowing 16
Love's Hand 17
Petal 18
Splendid Dance 19
Return 20

Contents

Section 2 21
Ancient Tone 23
Sighs and Whispers 24
Slow Steps 25
Wicked Dance 26
Blind in Your Love 27
Your Feet 28
Hush Mind 29
Write Me 30
Doll 31
Rude 32
Best and Worst 33
Precipice 34
Who Seeks? 35
No Self 36
Insane 37
No One 38
Unexpected 39
Restless Night 40
Morsel of Pain 41
I Wait 42
Gone Too Soon 43
Healing Heart 44
Lean on Me 45

Contents

Section 3 47
The Day...49
Stretched..50
Dissolved..51
Alone..52
Light in the Dark..53
Madwoman...54
Chasm...55
Changes..56
The Not-ness of Things 57
Crossroads 58
Imposter...60
Thousand Voices.. 61
You Move Away 62
Troubled Depths..63
Ease into Foregivable 64
Thunder 65
Divine of My Soul 66
Nightmare..67
Vast Sky..68
Ending Dance 69
Do Not Give Up...70
Dragon Flame 71
Wine...72
Shining Waves 73

Contents

Section 4 75
Wild Time of Night 77
That Light Touch 78
My Night 79
Thorns and Cutting Blades 80
Ecstatic Dance 81
Lost Taste 82
New Fruit 83
Arms 84
Green Mountain 85

Acknowledgements 87

Other books by Nicole Lawrence 89

Introduction

The poems in this book came about over the course of a few years. I don't feel I wrote them so much as they came through me. It was a flow of inspiration that felt like I was taking dictation.

In my twenties, I had a career working with horses and thought I'd spend the rest of my life doing that. Then, I experienced a loss that deeply affected me. Losing animals was part and parcel of working on a farm. I wasn't particularly close to this horse, yet his death had a profound impact that set me on a course of spiritual seeking.

As part of my spiritual journey, I returned to doing art, which I loved when I was younger. I moved around to different places, eventually landing in Hawai'i on the island of Kaua'i. As happens, life shifted. More and more, art became my focus. Around this time, I lost a number of people in a short amount of time, eight people in nine months. The losses included friends, both of my parents, and people who had touched my life in some way.

This much loss took time to work through. I finally emerged from my Persephone-like time in grief after nearly two years and discovered that my love for art had disappeared. I tried for a time to go back to it. I could remember how to paint, but any joy, desire, or passion for it was gone. A new cycle of spiritual seeking began, but on a deeper level than before. Most of these poems are from this time period and just after, where I discovered in myself a level of devotion I hadn't known existed.

One hopes to grow into expanded states of consciousness and freedom when on a spiritual path or following a spiritual discipline. I began experiencing these while facing some deep shadow and doing release work, as well as experiences that challenged and blew my mind. For many people, these experiences are short-lived visits into states that can be minutes, hours, days, or for some, months. At the time these poems came through to be written, I had been touching into and falling out of these states of bliss and ecstasy.

Pressures from the outside world produce their own challenges and distractions. I didn't have any support navigating these changes and did what I could, but eventually lost my way and landed back in the world operating from personalities and duality. Looking back, I realize it would have been helpful to have guidance to integrate the experiences I was having.

Without guidance and a firm foundation to build upon, these experiences for me remained a flash in the pan. However, at the time, they had a profound impact on me that continues to unfold to this day.

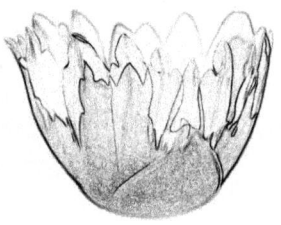

Section 1

Life Changing Hands

Life changing hands
Whose hands hold now
A life dissembling. Ecstasy
At all the little rips and tears
Of the known fabric of what is.
Wind of the unknown
Whistles through the gaps
Of fluttering memories
Opening, falling
I am the unknown.

Your Light

I walk into your light
Embrace me, fill me, enfold me
See through my eyes
Touch with my senses.

Transform this base into gold
Tune the vibration
Turn the compass
To face into your heart.

Moving Unseen

I sense you moving
Unseen, but felt,
Gifts received
From the All.

I watch your dance
You seek for
The All and
Take me with You.

Raise us up, Divine blaze
Burn with
Ecstatic embrace
We both flame and dissolve.

Hushed peace descends
No breath,
No sounds,
Waiting for the touch of one.

Expansion

Crashing are the waves of change,
Undone me and my little lives
Standing naked on the shore
Reborn to the heart's gift,
A silent night of whispers
And the acceptance of
Expansion to nowhere.

Gaze

Gaze of Your eyes.
They pierce me
and I dissolve.

Gone, but for
the looking back.
Inhale, exhale — one.

Truth is revealed.
Gently, all at once.
Transfixed in the gaze.

One loving One,
accepting all.
Ecstasy, bliss.

Held in stillness.
Trust, love, surrender.
You are All.

Heart Blossom

In the heat of the night
The heart will blossom.

A bud, waiting to open
It seeks the light.

Surroundings matter not
Nor circumstance.

Single guided, blinking back
From this hasty world.

It seeks its own refuge.
Yearning and nowhere to go.

Unravelling

The unraveling of all
That was known,
The certainty of being,
And sureness of place
In the universe.

The unquestioning
Of breathing in
And breathing out of
Day to day life,
Gone in an instant.

Free-fall into
The desert of non-existence.
So complete was
The alienation that
Loved ones flinched away.

I was a stranger to
Them and to myself.
I was nowhere,
No one, and they knew it
Before I did.

I became a ghost, a shade
in the shade of my life.
A fraud personified,
Going through the
Motions of life.

Cannot Go Back

What gift did you give me?
The end of that world -
How am I to deal with it?

What is done cannot be undone
What has been undone
Cannot be redone.

I cannot ever go back
To that ocean
in the sky, the wondering, the why.

Cares and the woes
Have gone to dust.
The mountain to climb
Is flat and still

What gift have you given me -
What freedom is this?
An end to all things and
No-thing simultaneously.

I am bereft and in awe
Of the split second
You changed everything
In that moment, none was ever the same.

Hour

In the hour
Of my darkness
You were there.
Stopping thought, stopping mind
From destruction of self.

Loved One

My Love, every cell
Craves for your touch
Ecstasy at your nearness,
Whispered breath,
Cradle of love,
Vastness beyond belief.

Tenderness eviscerates thought
I am open, helpless
In your bliss
Why continue to fight?
I long for total annihilation
In your love.

Tender Touch

Tender is your
Touch tonight.

A gentle caress
Unlocks wisdom.

Mighty thunder
Fades in the distance.

Rhythmic slow waves
Open universes and beyond.

Rocked in bliss
Memories, realities flee away.

Held in silence
Joy flows into ecstasy.

Wind of Unknowing

You come and you go,
Not really anywhere.
Forever giving, nurturing
Unseen, yet there,
Can this time I let you stay?
Where goes the flower
On the wind of unknowing?

Love's Hand

Love had a hand in it somewhere,
    I know.
Blind Love licking the ear of hearsay
    Tell, tell.
Faithful Love, kicking the dusty bones of sorrow
    Free, free.
Sheltered Love, embracing self-impalement on shards
    Feel, feel.
Insipid Love, demanding the marrow of all your 'morrows
    Never, never.
Carefree Love, lies in abandoned waiting
    Hopeful, hopeful.
Universal Love, expands its beating heart to beat mine
    Awake, awake.

Petal

Open me like a flower
Petal by petal
I fall at your feet
Beloved of God.

Lifted up
I drink air,
Touch sounds,
Taste sight.

Let me bloom forever,
Blazing glory of dissolving
Ashes floating, falling
New flowers being born.

Splendid Dance

Dance of splendid ecstasy
You do me in
My mind is confused
Struck dumb.

Dance of splendid ecstasy
Curve, twirl, set me free
Reach deep inside
Clear the path.

Dance of splendid ecstasy
Open me to your embrace
Leave no corner untouched
By your gentle grace.

Dance of splendid ecstasy
Consume, envelope, turn inside-out
This blessed flower
From your garden.

Return

Ahh friend, You found me
In my loneliness
And confusion.

Patiently You waited
Until my cemented gaze
Caught the flicker of
Your twinkling eye.

A slow approach
You, who I thought I knew,
Were new to me
All over again

Kindness on Your part
Imbued me with steadiness
Love flowed tenderly
Gentle heart opening.

The dam of caution broke
I was led like a lamb
Molded like clay
Given new life.

Ahh friend,
You found me again
There are no words
No end to the Dance.

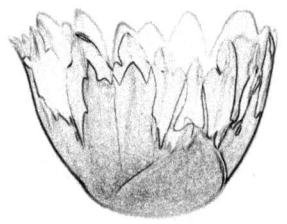

Section 2

Ancient Tone

An ancient tone from
The future calls
Causing all who hear it
To stop and pause.

Remembering a melody
Of Divine embrace from
Time beyond memory echoing grace
A song on the road home.

Sighs and Whispers

Sighs and whispers,
Of the night, somewhere
A snake is stirring
Consuming all.

Sighs and whispers,
Joy rises in its
Consuming embrace
Of fire.

Sighs and whispers,
Ghosts of the past
Evaporate, gone by
Her touch.

Sighs and whispers,
She frees the way
Expanding ripples in
The night.

Slow Steps

Be still in the night
The heart needs to speak.
An open embrace
Allows unfolding to matter.

Be cautious in this new dance
The steps are slow,
And curve through the universe
Like lightening on ice.

Be quiet in the night
Innocence is in awe of stars.
Alight in the Divine,
Second chances abound.

Be silent in the heart.
The courageous pave the way
Laughter dances with joy,
Tumbling down the starry night.

Wicked Dance

Share not the wicked dance
Go this way, then go that
Listen here, listen there
Somewhere Babylon is speaking.

Fools all listening to chatter.
Breathe in the dark night,
Fragrance of stillness surrounds,
Rest between here and there.

Blind in Your Love

I am blind in your love
How could I doubt
This glory?

Sensing You near
My breath steals away
The terrain is yours.

Inside me,
Nearer than my breath
I could miss you.

In Your love
You breathe me,
All else is gone.

Your Feet

I bow to your feet
Feet of All
Feet of One.

Blessed bliss
Walk into my heart
Leave Your imprint.

I am nothing
Without Your breath
Your life.

Created by Your hand
This life is nothing
But for Your Grace.

Touched I sigh, falling
Into Your ocean
Of silence.

Hush Mind

"Hush," you my mind
"Shhh," your busy inquiry
"Silence," your attitudes,
Let the Dance begin.

"Quiet," you who "knows"
"Be still," restless wanderer
"Stay calm," foreseer of anxieties,
Be taken away in swirls of ecstasy.

"Ohh," you who are afraid to die
"Ahh," you who never were
"Aum," who have never been,
Divine is All – Only Ever Is.

Write Me

Write me
Paint me
Curl me
Carve me.

Open me
Empty me
Fill me
Flow me.

Fire me
Strike me
Light me
Fan me.

Destroy me
Cleave me
Absorb me
Devour me.

Pierce me
Place me
Still me
Quiet me.

I am your play
Live in me
There is only One.

Doll

You bless me my friend
Pick me up, carry me
I am a doll in your arms.

The withered self
Folds its night shadows
At your approach.

Gone is the mystery
Of self-gone-mad
Insanity of ecstasy remains

I die in your embrace
Of impassioned love
Shameless expression of Divine.

Rude

I thought I was
going somewhere –
how rude of me.
Nowhere to go, no "where"
to get to.

I thought I could
talk to someone, get help
how rude of this world
the tricks it plays.
There is only the babbling of self.

Best and Worst

Deep in the night
Friend of darkness
You show me myself
My best and worst.

Under Your guidance
Tender and firm,
My eyes are opened
My secrets revealed.

Take my hand
Lift me up,
Though I resist
My heart hears all.

Show me truth that
Brings light
To the dark
And sets me free.

Circle my head
In Divine focus
As endless thoughts
Fall into eternity.

Precipice

Open mouthed I wait
You bring the next breath
Beating my heart
Life forges on.

Paused in the dance
I feel you stir,
Flowing waves
Envelope the shore.

I exhale, the next breath
Is Your doing,
On the precipice, life is Yours
Standing, falling, loving.

Who Seeks?

Who seeks to rush about?
Who seeks to change this or that?
Who wants to make it better?
Who desires to fix a worse?

Ghosts, running from pillar to post
Ghosts, seeking, searching, trying
Ghosts, moving this way and that
Ghosts, that heave, shove, and shift about.

In equanimity is being, beyond seeing.
In silence is patience, beyond waiting.
In stillness is peace, beyond all.
In the Peace, Is.

No Self

I look inside and see there
Is no me, no self.
Not there, never was
Is and isn't at
The same time.
A slight of mind
That allows personas
To be and do.

Insane

I think I am going insane
Quite insane,
A delightful insanity at that
What fun!

I do not know myself -
Gone away
What is this thing called self?
No one.

Did I ever really exist?
Who does?
None of it is real in the end.
Illusion, on illusion.

No One

Who is here?
No one
Who is inside?
No one
Who is that outside?
No one

Who said this?
No one
Who said that?
No one
Who looks and sees?
No one

Who is no one?
All One
Who speaks for no one?
All One
Who sees for no one?
All One

Who is inside?
All One
Who is that outside?
All One
Who is here?
One

Unexpected

I miss Your tender caress
And guiding ways
Revealing the me
That could not stay

Dissolved by Your touch.
Unexpected, this.
I did not know I was gone
And you could not "be," without a "me"

It was you and I,
The bliss of your embrace
And wonder of the adventure.
So safe you held me.

I know you for who you are
What a splendid journey
I reach for you and
It is myself.

Restless Night

Stars continue to shine
Yet my eyes have
Become shuttered,
Seeing illusion as real.

Where are you,
Trusted friend?
So much we shared,
So much you gave.

You disappeared in
The me of me,
In the I beyond I.

We are one
Yet I miss you
I miss falling down
At your feet.

Morsel of Pain

I want every morsel
Of this pain
Any reminder of you

Your life
Your death that
Is not death

Is this the ultimate
Separation,
Oneness that
Does away with each other?

There is again,
Only One, alone.
The pain is You.

I Wait

I wait, breathing
Lifeless life,
It is a comfort to think
I remain in your memory.

You set me down
Here, and
Lifted the veil
Why go on?

Gone Too Soon

My heart is heavy.
Why does the dance
Come close only to slip
Away again?

Is this the way of it?
Dance together
As one, then
Apart again?

Gone too soon
A connection of Spirit,
Light, substance
And Soul.

Healing Heart

Deep sorrow in my heart
There is only emptiness of
what once was filled.

Yet, the filling was an illusion
It had to cease.
Space that is empty is not space at all.

Uncertainty of unreality,
Illusion gone lost,
Considering itself All.

My friend you left, we left.
It had to be
Emptiness weeps.

Parting, truth is revealed.
You my healer, healing,
Always setting me free.

Lean on Me

How can I be gone?
I am in every wind,
In every song.
Lean on me forever,
I am always here,
Never there, away
Where you cannot reach.
There is only here
Where I Am.

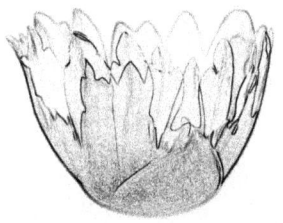

Section 3

The Day

Is this the day
When the shadows end?
The day I refuse to give in
To the victim voice within.

The day I lay down the lies
And become my own ally.
A day of sober consideration and
The end of outward pointed fingers.

This day is nigh on coming
A day without splendor.
But a day of a long
Reconning look in the mirror

A day without end,
The day I am my own friend,
A day of light-filled freedom
And endless possible futures.

Stretched

The awesome pain of being stretched,
Beyond limits, when there are none.

The freedom that burns bridges,
Looking back there can be no return

Memories, treasured and sad,
Now ashes in the wind of non-being.

Before: life was casting about in blindness,
Reaching for the unknown.

After: mattering doesn't matter, nowhere to reach to,
No one to reach or be reached.

What is left: a muddle of spare parts banging,
Clanking in diss-harmony down the road of eternity.

Dissolved

I am quite undone
By your medicines
Bitter, sweet, melancholic
Holes in my heart mended.

I gather to me the herbs of
Your magics every day
Courage, change, endurance,
And drink the draughts.

Your mysterious ways
Unlock, smooth,
Unruffle, set free
Chains of being break away.

I dance Your tunes and melodies
Outrageous, splitting, carefree.
In the All,
Dissolving, dissolved.

Alone

My heart hurts for Your touch
Your comfort,
The ease of Your being.

I don't want to put my feet
Down to walk on the hard,
Unyielding road without You.

Alone,
The vastness ahead waits
There is no joy here without You.

Walk I must, I know.
The ground uneven on the soles
Of my feet.

Small steps,
I don't want to leave
The place of our last embrace.

Light in the Dark

Light in the darkness
I lost sight of the glow,
Now, light barely shines at all,
Obscuring all is this veil.

Warm embrace of the cloying cloak
So safe, so normal, it all seems.
Sleep, blessed sleep,
Putting me to sleep.

I can no longer sense or feel You.
Asleep, I am held in thrall
To death's design of illusion
To die again and again.

Wake me! Reach me!
Smash this night
Razor my eyes open
Melt me in Your heart.

Burn away this darkness
Make me new
Keep me in Your keeping
Blessed always by Your touch.

Madwoman

Cursed I am
By the cursed mind
Chatter, chatter, chatter
There is a madwoman in my head.

Can you not hear her?
Natter, natter, natter
Grumbling to herself
Who is she? How did she get there?

Dissolve her my friend
Silence her shrieks
Consume her in Your ecstasy
Make a meal of her, won't You?

Then we can eat
Bliss together
I am her
I am Yours, at Your leisure.

Chasm

I look back and
See a life that is not mine,
Not the one I envisioned.
Spun out from who knows where
It ends at the canyon crevasse,
An impenetrable chasm.
Where none can cross, nor ever go back.

Changes

Change we must,
Change, change,
Change again
Until we bust.

Can't do this,
Can't do that.
First, it's this way
Then it's that.

Who can keep
This straight?
The stickman
In the night, might.

The puppeteer with
Broken strings
Tangles and untangles,
And the web grows.

Where will it cease?
These never-ending
Blackboard scratching
Night hieroglyphics.

Who will see the
Way out?
Who will clear
The clouds?

Beyond tomorrow
The new sun rises.
There is always
Hope for change.

The Not-Ness of Things

I wrestle with the
Not-ness of things.
The bigness, that isn't
The just-so, that won't
The sameness, that doesn't.

How can this be?
What is, isn't
What hasn't happened has
Already and always happened
Good is and isn't, at the same time.

Waves aren't waves
Sand isn't sand
They aren't anything else either
They just are and aren't
All the same.

How do I explain this?
Give words that aren't there
To concept-not-ness of eternity.
Awareness sublime is free from
Awareness at all.

Crossroads

My life feels like a crossroads,
To somewhere called nowhere.
From this silence
Stillness can speak.

A single waterfall
Down the cliff face,
The crossroads of
What was, what can be.

Teetering on this edge,
Heavy lidded.
The invitation to slip off in the
Oblivion of illusion is ever present.

Another life.
Stir the pot again
Death warmed over
A second serving.

Give in to the urge for familiar
Sleep and numb of oblivion?
Or stay on this razor's edge
Bound by timelessness?

Fears, judgements, and doubts.
Eat at the fringes of bone.
Trying to budge me from this stuck place.
The hollowing out never ceases.

Balancing on this precipice
Thorns of self-recrimination
Sting and bite.
They wake me up.

The stillness speaks
Opening its maw and
I stand silent,
Listening.

Imposter

An imposter reigns
Pretending to be whole
Pretending to be sane
Pretending all is right.

What once was
As easy as breathing
Is now dust that
Refuses to be born.

Why and where have
Met their end.
What have I gained?
Nothing stays the same.

Tomorrow doesn't exist
Yesterday is gone in a flame.
Yet the imposter remains,
Pretending none of it matters.

Thousand Voices

I open myself to
The All,
Breath of life
Pulse of reality.

Seeking the doorway out
Of the illusion of
Paper dreams and
Pretend existence.

Strewn in the heavens
Creations abound
Finding comfort
From each other.

Alone in the night
I set my cry free,
Thousands of voices
Respond in kind.

They are who I am,
Inseparable companions
Of mute and silent
Dances, circling along.

Boundaryless and beyond all being
The are and
Are not.
I am not, and Am.

You Move Away

I feel you in the night
Coming near.
I reach for you
You move away.

Stirring in the dark
I ache for you
Come to me
My Self Divine.

Troubled Depths

As the day draws to a close
I am troubled.

Light shifts, life relaxes
Something in me stills, holding its breath.

People hurry home, joining together
In my depths, I cry mute tears.

The hush of twilight descends,
I wait, wondering.

The day's endings announce themselves,
I am a foreigner in a foreign land.

Unrelenting is the fall of night
I weep, lost.

Ease Into Unforgivable

I Feel flawed with no way
To soothe it.
I lost myself in life's sorrows.

Fell for the play of illusion
Grim grins allowing
Nothing to show.

I have lost
my very breath, it seems.
Gone is the connection with You

I wait, transfixed in the
Moment of hell
Between possibilities.

I know I must go on
To walk on broken wings
And the wrench of dry bones.

Self-incarceration and banishment,
Does not abate the waves
Of mud brown sorrow.

My carelessness condemned me
To wait, hoping to take another breath
And ease into the forgivable.

Thunder

Roaring thunder come and
Take me away.
The dew of the dawn light
Cannot hold a candle to your night.

I am helpless in your waves
Smashed to the shore
Roll me until
You are finished your work.

Allow me no breath to breathe
End my singular existence
Lower me in vats of golden light
Choke me into life, by your night.

Pry open the crevasses
That keep separation alive
Undo my doing and not-doing
Divining your light in the night.

Divine of My Soul

Divine of my Soul
Devotion falls at your feet
Consumed in bliss
Radiance fills all.

Nightmare

Haunted I was by
My nightmare.
Life unraveled,
Weaving dead threads
Of illusion.

Emptiness in my
Hands, passions became
Air that suffocated,
My Soul undone
Wavering, waiting.

Your touch intervenes
Life waking after pain.
Alive! I
Live yet again,
Another chance.

I have become ashes
Blown out
On the breath of
The endlessly
Changing dance.

Vast Sky

Vast is the sky of night,
Infinity forever moving
At the speed of light
Beyond the bounds of sight.

Crying me awake
Stars fall like tears
Enlivening me with their
Whispers and secrets beyond my
fears.

Beyond the reachable
The past is gone,
The present inconceivable
Meaning tries to have life of its own.

In the dark find the thread
And gather courage for the
Changes in the night ahead
That allow the greater to be.

Ending Dance

The ending dance
On the high precipice
Standing the edge,
Arms pinwheeling —
Fall in?
Fall out?

Fall in — unknown insanity,
Fall out — known insanity,
The edge yawns, inviting,
Numb forgetfulness is gone
There is no
Turning back.

Sheer fortitude takes the plunge.
Only endlessly circling rats
With bloodied noses
Are ready to die.
Let go, let go
How bad can insanity be?

Do Not Give Up

Do not give up my dear,
You are so close
Your bereavement leaves you
Open like paving stones.

It will soon be time to rise
From the burial grounds of self-shame,
To take the leave of the sucking mud,
To stand at the precipice naked.

You have not lost anything,
You have become undone, untainted,
Grieve the loss of self
Grieve the old substance of the past.

Let the pale ale of sorrow
Spark you awake
Give in, not to sadness
But to the change.

Let the pain have you, make you new
Bow under the soft skies of grief
Let remorse hammer you a new heart,
Inhale the ashes of futility, get new lungs.

I am with you all the way
To the stars and back
Forged on the anvil of the Divine
Let yourself be new.

Dragon Flame

Gone into the fires
Of turmoil and pain
Love lost, but life gained.

Freedom from without
A new charge within
A chance encounter on the wind?

Fear not the looping
Dragon snares of flame where
Small minds think all the same.

Freedom lurks anew, anew
Gouging deep furrows in
The mind's hidden burrows.

Opening to the sweet nectar
Of release and bliss
Going home you cannot miss.

Wine

Drink me in
Love Divine
I am wine on
Your lips, tasting All.

With gentle caress
Open that which
Is All Yours
Melting, beyond the sun.

Agony, ecstasy
They are your servants
Dead I am to
All but Your touch.

Guide me, use me
I fall into
Your breath and
Loving, sublime nature.

Shining Waves

Dance me till I die
Erase and erase again
The me of divided I.
Swallow whole these
Burning coals of memories.

Spread wings and fly,
The sun is not enough
To burn the dross.
The stars remain unmoved
Shallow passions, spark and die.

Dive down the shadowed slope
Speed and speed,
The bye gone-gone frees
Flight-clipped birds
Who sing and soar.

Freedom comes in death
Of conditioned self.
In the life that is beyond,
Radiance flourishes, revealing
Unbounded shining waves of light.

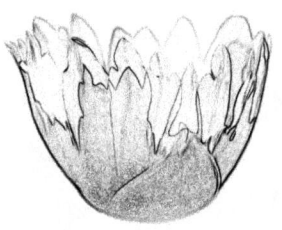

Section 4

Wild Time of Night

I am up in the wild time of the night.
The time when dew magically forms
On leaves and hangs on the underside of
Twigs in pregnant drops.

The wild time of night when the sun
May decide not to come up again.
The time when change can happen
And arms reach for shores unknown,
Yet felt in that wild night.

When freedom is possible, but not promised.
When all that is known, is dropped in an instant
For a different destination
In the wild time of the night.

The time wolves know the moon and
Stars bend down to kiss the lakes.
And the light that sees all,
Sees, in the wild time of night.

Mountains climb the heavens
In the wild time of night
And winds whisper of still waters
In the deep of star-kissed lakes.

The wild time of the night
When all is asleep and awake.

That Light Touch

Your light touch, barely there
Everything changed.
A blazing column of light
Revealing, all is alive,
All is aware.
Love pressing upon Love.

Radiant sun of intensity
Ecstatic rain of oneness.
Bliss of being,
Embraced in Love
Lost to time
Stillness breathes All.

My Night

Set aside your day
For my night
Let me draw
The dawn breath from you.

Collapse into the
Rubble of unreality.
Dry and dying,
Life's meaning passes.

Oblivion awaits in
This cure for the illusion.
Die to the sleepy sun
Sink into muck.

Be washed clean
By the depths.
Intensity turned inside out,
Love circles again.

Emerge from the turmoil
Tasting blood and freedom
Cowards back away and fall
Over the precipice of apathy.

Thorns and Cutting Blades

Bliss is yours my friend
I am at your mercy
Frail nights dwindle away
Caressing as they leave.

A trail of bitter taste
Is sweet on my lips
Your Divine power consumes
All poisons, reverses the kill.

Freedom comes at your
Blessing touch. Gentle, probing
I am twisted free of
Thorns and cutting blades.

Free me again and again
Surrender my unyielding core
To your fire of
Anguished delight to nothingness.

Ecstatic Dance

What is this ecstatic dance?
Can you not love me enough?
Love drives the dead life
Out of me.
Let me die awake
In your endless embrace.

Lost Taste

I have lost my
Taste for this world.
No longer can I
Believe in the "buzz."

Soup without flavor,
It is bland, the
Old possibilities
No longer real.

Things of the world
Don't capture me as they once did.
Contentment rests
In the silence.

New Fruit

A new tree grows in the
Garden of my heart.
Bearing fruit that
Brings a fresh start.

Once a fleeting spark in the
Dark is now a lamp lit
With a steady flame.
A reason to begin again.

Peace in the heart that
Quiets the mind.
Old shadows rise to blind
But quickly fade.

Within the tree's benevolence
A quiet embrace of life in balance.
In the silence joy abounds and
Presence surrounds.

Arms

I have arms
Waiting for me
Across the
Great divide.

The love
Left behind
On this
World's journey.

Waits and watches
For my return
The veil
To cross.

The high arched
Bridge half-stands
Step off
And trust.

A welcome celebration
Of joyous homecoming
Quiet sigh
Love's embrace.

Green Mountain

I climbed the green mountain
Paused at the precipice to look back.

The valley, alight with gaiety behind me.
Life, light, the story unfolding.

From this height the dance
Goes on without me.

Beyond the dance,
stretches infinity.

An ocean of stars with a
Dance hall of life in its midst.

I cannot go back
The unknown of the downhill side waits.

I pause at the rim, look back to view the light,
Turn and step over the edge.

Acknowledgements

First, I'd like to thank my publishers and friends, Bonnie Groessl and Mike Dauplaise, for believing in me when I came up with this totally different project from what I normally do.

Thank you, Jean Marie McEntee, for your valuable insight and feedback on the rough draft, and for being there for me when the Universe was rolling the dice while the ship was tilting in the approaching storm.

Thank you, Vima Lamura, for your encouragement, and hours of listening to me read these poems over the phone so I could hear the power in my own voice, and for coming with your pearl mala and chanting mantras in the worst of the storm.

Thank you, Julia Hall, for your encouragement and feedback on the manuscript, and for the wonderful honey from Alaska I used in my chai while working on the book.

Thank you, secret angels, dressed as all the doctors, nurses, and healthcare workers in what was a challenging year.

Namaskaram and thank you, Sadhguru, for arriving in my life at just the right time and for your teachings that help build a firm foundation for a blissful life. Namaskaram and thank you to all the Isha volunteers around the world who work in concert to bring Sadhguru's wisdom to the world.

Other Books by H. Nicole Lawrence

Doors to Transformation:
My Mother - My Self

Nicole helps readers who may be struggling with their own childhood experiences by sharing her story of forgiveness and describing the tools that contributed to her healing journey. The transformational process includes coming to peace with the past as well as actively working toward releasing emotions so you can become the person you want to be.

World in a Shoe:
My Journey with Horses

Nicole takes you on an intimate journey with horses and the people around them who touched her life, giving her a greater understanding of human nature and herself.

Kukui:
The Art of Designed Nut Leis

Nicole uses her expertise in painting and beaded jewelry making to identify effective techniques for making beautiful kukui leis – the Hawaiian word for a garland or necklace. This easy-to-follow guide includes instruction and tips for hobbyists and artists of any ability level to wood-burn, dye, and paint kukui nuts, while gaining an appreciation for Hawaiian culture and the history of kukui trees and their nuts.

www.ingramcontent.com/pod-product-compliance
Lightning Source LLC
Chambersburg PA
CBHW070653050426
42451CB00008B/333